HELEN **KELLER**

Educator, Activist & Author

BY VALERIE BODDEN

CONTENT CONSULTANT
GRAHAM WARDER, PHD
ASSOCIATE PROFESSOR OF HISTORY
KEENE STATE COLLEGE

Essential Library

An Imprint of Abdo Publishing | abdopublishing.com

abdopublishing.com

Published by Abdo Publishing, a division of ABDO, PO Box 398166, Minneapolis, Minnesota 55439. Copyright © 2017 by Abdo Consulting Group, Inc. International copyrights reserved in all countries. No part of this book may be reproduced in any form without written permission from the publisher. Essential Library™ is a trademark and logo of Abdo Publishing.

Printed in the United States of America, North Mankato, Minnesota
022016
092016

Cover Photo: RK/AP Images, cover
Interior Photos: AP Images, 4, 91; Bettmann/Corbis, 9, 25, 30, 44, 59, 66, 74, 81, 86, 94; Everett Collection, 11, 63, 79; GraphicaArtis/Corbis, 12; Library of Congress, 16, 32, 41, 56; PhotoQuest/Getty Images, 19; William Notman/Library of Congress, 22; Boston Pictoral Archive, Boston Public Library, 35; Courtesy of Perkins School for the Blind Archives, Watertown, MA, 47; Haines Photo Co./Library of Congress, 50-51; Hulton-Deutsch Collection/Corbis, 53, 55; Time Life Pictures/Pix Inc./The LIFE Picture Collection/Getty Images, 70; Underwood & Underwood/Corbis, 76

Editor: Melissa York
Series Designer: Becky Daum

Cataloging-in-Publication Data

Names: Bodden, Valerie, author.
Title: Helen Keller: educator, activist & author / by Valerie Bodden.
Description: Minneapolis, MN : Abdo Publishing, [2017] | Series: Essential lives |
    Includes bibliographical references and index.
Identifiers: LCCN 2015959854 | ISBN 9781680782998 (lib. bdg.) |
    ISBN 9781680774795 (ebook)
Subjects: LCSH: Keller, Helen, 1880-1968--Juvenile literature. | Deafblind
    women--United States--Biography--Juvenile literature. | Deafblind people--
    United States--Biography--Juvenile literature.
Classification: DDC 362.4/1092 [B]--dc23
LC record available at http://lccn.loc.gov/2015959854

CONTENTS

CHAPTER
ONE

MYSTERY REVEALED

Helen Keller stood in the garden behind her family's house on April 5, 1887. The six-and-a-half-year-old could not see the butterflies flitting from flower to flower. She could not hear the birds calling to one another across the yard. But she could smell the violets and the lilies, the grasses and the berries, that grew there. She quivered as the breeze slid over her arms and through her hair. She felt the vibrations of a world in motion. But she could not put words to all her sensations.

For five years, she had been deaf and blind, locked inside her own head, with no ability to communicate with the world around her. But her family had recently hired a young woman named Annie Sullivan as Helen's teacher. At first, Helen did not like her teacher. As she stood in the garden with Sullivan, she still was not sure she did.

At age seven, Helen Keller had recently learned how to communicate with others.

Communicating with Fingers

Almost from the moment of her arrival, Sullivan had been moving her fingers in different patterns in Helen's hand. Helen quickly learned to repeat the patterns. But she did not yet understand that each of Sullivan's movements represented a letter of the manual alphabet, which was used to communicate with people who were deaf and blind. She did not realize the patterns of letters made words or that the words named the objects around her.

All Helen knew was that repeating certain patterns brought rewards. If she repeated the pattern she had learned for *cake*, for example, she might get a piece of cake. When she wanted a drink, she might use the pattern she had learned for *mug* or the one she had learned for *water*. She did not realize

SMELL AND TOUCH

In the absence of sight and hearing, Helen relied on her senses of smell and touch. Sullivan reported that Helen could identify several flowers simply by their scents. She could distinguish between different kinds of roses and various varieties of mushrooms. Once she even recognized someone with whom she had corresponded but never met—he smelled like the tobacco he used, which had left its scent on the letters he wrote her. Helen could interpret the vibrations made by clapping, walking, and even the rustle of papers falling to the floor. She could recognize friends simply by the touch of their hands.

these words meant two separate things—one stood for the vessel and one for the liquid inside.

Just that morning, Helen's teacher had tried again to teach her the difference between *water* and *mug*. When Helen still did not grasp it, the teacher let the young girl play. But she tried to use playtime as a learning experience, too. Helen was playing with a new doll, so Sullivan spelled the letters *d-o-l-l* into her hand. Then she handed Helen her old rag doll and again spelled *d-o-l-l* into her hand, hoping to teach her that the word *doll* was the name of both objects. Frustrated, Helen

THE MANUAL ALPHABET

Invented by medieval Spanish monks wanting to communicate without breaking their vows of silence, the manual alphabet is a way of forming letters with the fingers of one hand. By the 1700s, the manual alphabet had been adopted in France to communicate with the deaf. In the 1830s, seven-year-old Laura Bridgman of the United States became the first deaf-blind individual to learn the manual alphabet.

While the manual alphabet for the deaf is signed into the air, the manual alphabet for the deaf-blind is signed into the person's hand. To form the letter *a*, for example, a person touches the tip of the deaf-blind person's thumb. The letter *b* is made by putting all the fingertips together and placing them in the person's palm.

People who regularly communicated with Keller using the manual alphabet became very fast, spelling into her hand as quickly as a person could type on a typewriter. As she felt their fingers move, Keller said, she did not register individual letters but entire words and sentences.

threw her new doll across the room, and it shattered. She was pleased to have made her point.

Water!

Now, in the garden, Sullivan led Helen to the water pump. She gave Helen her mug and held her hand under the spout. As the cold liquid splashed over Helen's fingers, Sullivan spelled *w-a-t-e-r* into her other hand again and again. Helen froze, startled. Suddenly, she understood. The letters *w-a-t-e-r* meant "the wonderful cool something that was flowing over my hand."[1]

Helen realized for the first time that this word referred not only to the liquid rushing over her hand but also to the liquid that filled lakes and rivers and oceans. And she understood *mug* was the name of a container that could hold water or other liquids and that mugs could be all sorts of shapes and sizes—and the same name could be used for all of them.

With that realization, Helen said, "somehow the mystery of language was revealed to me," and it "awakened my soul, gave it light, hope, joy, set it free!"[2] Suddenly, she understood that everything had a name, and she wanted to know the name of everything. All the way back to the house, she made Sullivan spell to her

Visitors to Helen's childhood home can still see the water pump where Helen unlocked the secret of language.

the names of every object and action she encountered: *teacher*, *baby*, *door*, *open*, *shut*, *give*, *go*, *come*. By the end of the day, she had learned 30 new words.[3]

A New Person

When she returned to the house, Helen remembered the doll she had broken earlier in the day. She ran over to find the broken pieces. Earlier, she had not felt bad about breaking the doll. But now, for the first time, she was sorry. She cried when she could not put the doll back together.

As she later explained, before Sullivan came to her, "I did not know that I am. I lived in a world that was

HELEN KELLER IN FILM

The 1962 movie *The Miracle Worker* portrayed the early relationship between Helen Keller and Sullivan, culminating with the scene at the water pump. Screenwriter William Gibson based the movie on his 1959 Broadway play of the same name, which was itself based on Keller's autobiography, *The Story of My Life*. In both the play and the movie, Anne Bancroft played Sullivan, while Patty Duke played Keller. Both actresses won Academy Awards for their performances. *The Miracle Worker* was remade for television in 1979, with Patty Duke now playing Sullivan. It was remade again by Disney in 2000. Today, Gibson's original play is still performed each summer on the grounds of Keller's childhood home.

a no-world. . . . I had neither will nor intellect."[4] But now that she could put a name to the world around her, she was like a "radiant fairy," Sullivan reported.[5] Before that day, Helen had been unwilling to show Sullivan affection. But that night, the little girl curled up with her teacher in bed and kissed her for the first time. The next morning, she darted around the room, asking Sullivan to spell to her the name of everything she touched and kissing her teacher with joy for every new word she learned.

From that day forward, Helen's desire to learn never flagged. She would go on to become the first deaf-blind person to complete a college education. She would become a famous writer, honest public speaker, and tireless champion for the blind and

Helen, *left*, would remain close to Sullivan, *right*, for the rest of her teacher's life.

visually impaired. And through it all, she would change the world's perceptions of what a person with disabilities could accomplish.

CHAPTER
TWO

TEACHER

Helen was born on June 27, 1880, in the rural town of Tuscumbia, Alabama. She was the first child of Captain Arthur Henley Keller and his wife, Kate. Kate was 20 years younger than her husband, who had served as a captain in the Confederate army during the American Civil War (1861–1865) and afterward edited a local newspaper. When Helen was five, Arthur Keller was appointed US marshal for the Northern District of Alabama. US marshals enforce the law for federal courts and represent the US government.

"The beginning of my life was very simple, and very much like the beginning of every other little life," Helen later wrote, "for I could see and hear when I first came to live in this beautiful world."[1] Helen was a bright and energetic baby, and according to her mother, by the time she was six months old she could say "How d'ye" and "tea, tea, tea." She said "wah-wah" for water.[2] By the time she was one year old, she had begun walking.

Helen was young enough when she lost her sight and hearing that later in life she had no memory of using those senses.

Helen's parents adored their baby, with her fine curls, blue eyes, and easy affection.

But in February 1882, when Helen was 19 months old, she fell ill with what doctors at the time called brain fever. Modern-day doctors believe the illness could have been scarlet fever, meningitis, or rubella, all of which can cause similar permanent complications. As her body temperature spiked, Helen's doctor warned the family she might die. But after several days, the fever came down.

Although Helen's parents were overjoyed by their daughter's recovery, they soon realized something was wrong. Helen did not blink when her parents waved their hands in front of her face. Nor did she respond to the sound of their voices or loud noises. The fever had left the little girl deaf and blind. Helen later said that when she woke up from her illness and discovered that it was still dark, she must have wondered

HELEN'S FRIEND

After losing her sight and hearing, Helen passed many of her days with Martha Washington, the daughter of the Kellers' cook. Although Martha was a few years older than Helen, she usually let Helen have her way—otherwise, Helen might hit her. The two young girls helped in the kitchen, fed the hens and turkeys, and searched for guinea fowl eggs.

why the night was so long. But, she said, "Gradually I got used to the silence and darkness that surrounded me and forgot that it had ever been different."[3]

Locked In

Stuck in a dark and silent world, Helen took to sitting in her mother's lap or hanging about her legs as she worked around the house. Since she could not hear other people speaking, she did not learn any new words, and soon even the few words she had learned before losing her hearing were forgotten—all except "wah-wah."[4] But over time, Helen developed her own signs to communicate with her family. A head shake meant *no* and a pull on the hand meant *come*. She would pretend to slice and butter bread when she wanted bread to eat. She understood when her mother wanted her to fold the laundry or run to get something.

But this basic form of communication was not enough for Helen. She often grew frustrated by her inability to get her point across, and she began acting out. She threw wild tantrums, hitting, scratching, and biting her parents and anyone who got too close. She would throw dishes and lamps, stick her hands into other people's food at the dinner table, and pinch

Throughout her life, Helen used her awareness of her surroundings to perform chores and other tasks.

her grandmother. When she was five, her mother gave birth to another little girl, Mildred. Jealous of her sister, Helen overturned the cradle. Fortunately, her mother caught the baby. By the time Helen was six, she was throwing tantrums almost hourly. She felt no remorse for her behavior—she had no way to understand how it hurt those around her.

Helen's family did not know how to handle her outbursts. They felt sorry for the little girl and were unwilling to discipline her. Some family members insisted the girl was unmanageable and should be institutionalized. But Helen's parents refused to send her away.

TABLE MANNERS

Shortly after Sullivan's arrival, she decided she had to stop Helen from eating everyone else's food. So one morning she refused to let Helen steal any of her breakfast. When Helen threw a tantrum, Sullivan continued eating. The little girl pinched her teacher, who slapped her hand away. Finally, Helen sat down and began to eat with her fingers. Sullivan put a spoon in her hand, but Helen threw it to the floor. Sullivan made her pick it up and try again until Helen finished her meal using the spoon. Next, Sullivan struggled for an hour to make Helen fold her napkin. Finally, that was done, and she allowed Helen to leave the room.

A Ray of Hope

Then Kate read Charles Dickens's *American Notes for General Circulation*, in which the British author had recounted an 1842 trip to the Perkins Institution, a school for the blind in Boston, Massachusetts. He wrote about meeting Laura Bridgman, a young girl who had become deaf and blind at age two. Dr. Samuel Gridley Howe of the institution had educated her using the manual language. Suddenly, Kate felt a ray of hope. Perhaps Helen could be educated, too. But Howe had been dead for more than ten years. And Boston was far from Tuscumbia.

As the Kellers pondered the possibility of getting an education for Helen, they continued seeking a medical cure for their daughter's ailments. They brought her to a specialist in Baltimore, Maryland, but he said nothing could be done to improve Helen's eyesight or hearing. He recommended they consult with Alexander Graham Bell, an expert in deafness, about how best to educate Helen.

Bell, whose mother and wife were both deaf, had invented the telephone in 1876 in the hope it could be used as a sort of hearing aid. Afterward, he pursued other ways to help the deaf. He recommended the Kellers contact Michael Anagnos, the new director of the Perkins Institution. Helen's father took Bell's advice and wrote to Anagnos at once, inquiring if he had a

Helen with Alexander Graham Bell in 1901

teacher who could begin Helen's education. Anagnos
soon responded: he did.

"Soul's Birthday"

Anagnos's top pick for the job was Sullivan, a recent
graduate from the Perkins Institution who was partially
blind. Sullivan was only 21 years old, but she had studied
Dr. Howe's methods of educating the deaf-blind and had
spent many hours visiting Bridgman and communicating
with her using the manual alphabet. Anagnos knew she
was a fiery Irish woman who did not give up easily.

Sullivan arrived in Tuscumbia on March 3, 1887, a
day Helen would later celebrate as her "soul's birthday."[5]

Sullivan was surprised by the six-year-old's appearance. "Somehow I had expected to see a pale, delicate child," she wrote to a friend. "But there's nothing pale or delicate about Helen. She is large, strong, and ruddy, and as unrestrained in her movements as a young colt. . . . Her face . . . is intelligent, but lacks mobility, or soul, or something."[6]

The same day she arrived, Sullivan began teaching her new pupil the manual alphabet, and over the next several days, Helen learned to spell a number of words,

ANNIE SULLIVAN

Born on April 14, 1866, in Feeding Hills, Massachusetts, Annie Sullivan grew up in poverty. When she was young, she developed trachoma, a disease that led to partial blindness. Her mother died when she was eight years old, and afterward, her father abandoned his children. Sullivan and her younger brother moved to a poorhouse, where her brother soon died. After four years in the poorhouse, Sullivan insisted that she receive an education. She began to study at the Perkins Institution, where she excelled, graduating at the top of her class in 1886. While she was at Perkins, she underwent two eye operations, which partially restored her sight.

When Anagnos asked if she would be interested in teaching Helen, Sullivan at first doubted she would be able to handle the assignment. She returned to the Perkins Institution, where she spent six months reviewing the methods used to instruct Laura Bridgman. She later said she had no high ideals when she took the job as Helen's teacher; she simply needed the money. But she became Helen's closest friend and dedicated the rest of her life to her student.

including *pin*, *hat*, *cup*, *sit*, *stand*, and *walk*. But she did not understand how to use the words.

A Hard Lesson

Although Helen was now learning new ways to communicate, her behavior did not improve. She often struggled against her teacher, once locking Sullivan in her room and another time knocking out one of Sullivan's front teeth. Sullivan realized she needed to teach Helen obedience before she could educate her. She knew Helen's family was unwilling to discipline the child, so she asked for permission to take Helen to stay in a little cottage on the other side of the Kellers' garden. Helen's parents would be allowed to check on their daughter, but they could not let her know they were there. Reluctantly, the Kellers agreed.

At first, Sullivan struggled to get Helen to obey her simplest requests, such as getting dressed. But after a week, Helen had become gentle and obedient. She and Sullivan soon moved back into the main house. Now it was time for Sullivan to get down to the real work of educating her pupil.

CHAPTER
THREE

LOVE OF LEARNING

With Helen's behavior under control, Sullivan focused on teaching her new words. After the April 5 breakthrough at the water pump, Helen's vocabulary expanded rapidly. By the end of June, she knew more than 400 words.[1]

Sullivan knew babies acquire language by listening as it is constantly spoken around them. Believing the same method could be used for Helen, she decided to "talk into [Helen's] hand as we talk into the baby's ears."[2] All day long, she spelled to Helen, telling her what she saw, what was happening around them, what others were doing—anything she could think of. As she spelled, she used whole sentences and did not stop to explain new words. She knew Helen would not understand much of what she spelled at first. But she could guess the meaning of some words through context. And others she would pick up over time.

Instead of sitting in a schoolroom and following a regular schedule of lessons, Helen and Sullivan spent

Sullivan stayed at Helen's side so she could sign to her what was going on around them.

most days outdoors, where they would talk about whatever interested Helen. Soon, Helen learned the names of the trees surrounding her home. She fingered birds' nests and held frogs as they croaked. She stroked the delicate wings of butterflies and smelled the clover-laced breath of the ponies in the barn. Through it all, Helen constantly asked questions of her teacher, always eager to learn more.

TOUGH LOVE

Although Helen loved her teacher dearly, some people close to the two feared Sullivan was too hard on her student. If she caught Helen slacking in her work, Sullivan would refuse to speak to her. To keep Helen from biting her nails, Sullivan tied her hands behind her back, leaving Helen unable to communicate. When Helen proved to be no good at sculpting, Sullivan slapped her face with a slab of wet clay. Yet afterward she would always apologize—and Helen was always the first to defend her teacher against accusations of wrongdoing.

Reading and Writing

Only a few months after Helen learned her first word, Sullivan decided it was time to teach her to read. She started by using cards printed with raised letters. She placed Helen's fingers on each letter while at the same time spelling that letter into Helen's other hand. Within a day, Helen learned to read all the letters. She soon learned to read braille as well.

Helen found great joy in her new ability to read and spent

Helen developed a lifelong love of reading.

several hours each day with her books, paging through them to find all the words she knew. By May 1887, she was reading simple children's stories, and she soon progressed to more complicated literature, including the Bible and the works of playwright William Shakespeare. For Helen, books were a world in which her disabilities did not hold her back. As she later said, "Literature is my

Utopia. . . . No barrier of the senses shuts me out from the sweet, gracious discourse of my book-friends."[3]

Shortly after Helen learned to read, Sullivan taught her to write using a grooved writing board, into which she pressed a sheet of paper. The grooves of the board were like lines on a sheet of paper, and they helped Helen write straight across the page. She held her pencil with her right hand and used her left hand to help shape and space the letters. Helen began writing letters to family members and friends, a habit she would maintain for the rest of her life.

Sweet and Loving

As the world of learning opened to Helen, her behavior rapidly improved. Although she still threw occasional tantrums, for the most part she was sweet and loving. Sullivan also taught Helen to laugh—something she had done little of since losing her hearing. Sullivan tickled Helen and taught her to swing, tumble, jump, and skip.

As Helen's lessons continued, she grew closer to her teacher. Although Helen conversed with her parents, who had both learned the manual language, Sullivan insisted on being the only one to teach Helen new words. Helen thrived under Sullivan's guidance, and by the end of 1887, she felt, "My teacher is so near to me that I scarcely think of myself apart from her."[4]

The Perkins Institution

In May 1888, Helen, her mother, and Sullivan traveled north to Boston to visit the students at the Perkins Institution. On the way, they were invited to meet President Grover Cleveland. This was the first of Helen's presidential visits. From this time on, she would meet every president in office during her lifetime.

They arrived at the Perkins Institution on May 26. Helen was thrilled to discover most of the girls there knew the manual alphabet and could talk with her. In addition to making new friends, Helen spent hours in the institution's library, with its shelves full of embossed and braille books.

EMBOSSED OR BRAILLE

In general, books for the blind fall into two categories: embossed books with roman letters in raised print, or braille books, which use patterns of dots to indicate letters. During Helen's lifetime, books for the blind were limited because they were expensive to publish. Helen had greater access to such books than most visually impaired people because of her connection with the Perkins Institution. In addition, a number of her friends had braille or embossed books made just for her. Among Helen's favorite books were the Bible and *Little Lord Fauntleroy* by Frances Hodgson Burnett.

That summer, Helen, her mother, and Sullivan spent time on Cape Cod in Massachusetts, at the home of Sophia Hopkins, with whom Sullivan had lived for a time while she was attending the Perkins Institution. There, Helen had her first feel and taste of the sea. After being knocked down by a wave, she struggled to her feet and spelled, "Who put salt in the water?"[5]

In September, Helen and Sullivan returned to the Perkins Institution for two months before heading back to Tuscumbia, where Sullivan continued Helen's lessons. Helen was now studying reading, arithmetic, geography, and zoology. The strain of constantly reading to her student hurt Sullivan's eyes, and in the summer of 1889, she traveled alone to Boston to seek medical treatment. It was the first time Helen had been away from her teacher since Sullivan's arrival two years earlier, and she struggled to cope.

When Sullivan returned in the fall, she and Helen again traveled to Perkins, where they would spend much of the next three winters. Helen was considered a guest of the school rather than a regular student, but she joined the other children for classes in arithmetic, earth science, zoology, music, French, basketry, and clay modeling.

Finding Fame

In 1888, Anagnos published a paper calling Helen a "second Laura Bridgman."[6] He wrote, "Of all the blind and deaf-mute children, Helen Keller of Tuscumbia, Alabama, is undoubtedly the most remarkable. It is no hyperbole to say that she is a phenomenon. . . . In view of all the circumstances her achievements are little short of a miracle."[7] Anagnos's report drew attention from around the country. The public was used to thinking of people with disabilities as somehow defective. But

MEETING HER HERO

Almost from the time she learned to communicate, Helen was fascinated by the story of Laura Bridgman. Bridgman had lost her sight and hearing at age two due to scarlet fever. Her senses of taste and smell had been affected as well. Around the age of seven, she was sent to the Perkins Institution, where she was taught the manual alphabet. As the first deaf-blind person to receive an education, she became famous. Although she learned to communicate, Bridgman never learned to cope with the world around her and remained at the Perkins Institution for the rest of her life.

On Helen's first visit to Perkins in 1888, she had an opportunity to meet Bridgman, to whom she had often been compared. But Helen found the 60-year-old deaf-blind woman cold and dull, like a statue she had once felt in a garden. For her part, Bridgman was taken aback by the boisterous young Helen. The older woman refused to let Helen touch her face or the lace she was working on because she feared the girl's hands were dirty. Bridgman died at the Perkins Institution in 1889.

Laura Bridgman's education laid the groundwork
for many of Helen's early lessons.

here was a young deaf-blind girl who not only seemed to be a prodigy but also showed a special "sweetness of disposition," according to Anagnos's report.[8]

Newspapers everywhere printed pictures of Helen posing with her teacher or sitting alone with a braille book on her lap. Reporters traveled to Tuscumbia to learn more about the young girl, and news of her achievements impressed even Queen Victoria in England. Many writers and academics were associated with the Perkins Institution, and Helen had soon met the poets John Greenleaf Whittier and Oliver Wendell Holmes, as well as author and clergyman Phillips Brooks. Brooks so impressed her that she later asked her parents to name her baby brother after him.

Soon, however, newspapers began exaggerating Helen's achievements. According to some reports, she could speak fluently, play the piano, and demonstrate geometric principles with toy blocks. Sullivan grew frustrated with such reports. "The truth is not wonderful enough to suit the newspapers," she wrote, "so they enlarge upon it and invent ridiculous embellishments."[9] Such embellishments only served to fuel public skepticism over Helen's true achievements.

CHAPTER
FOUR

THE DREAM OF SPEAKING

Although Helen could communicate fluently by means of the manual language, she knew others communicated using their mouths. One day she asked her teacher about this: "How do the blind girls know what to say with their mouths? Why do you not teach me to talk like them? Do deaf children ever learn to speak?"[1] Sullivan explained that some deaf children learned to speak by watching others move their mouths. But because Helen could not see, she could not do that.

The movement to teach deaf people to speak, known as oralism, was highly controversial at the time. One of its strongest supporters was Alexander Graham Bell, who thought sign language was a barbaric form of communication. Many in the deaf community who had achieved great success by using sign language resented Bell's interference. Helen, however, insisted she wanted to communicate in the same way as those who could

Helen learned to read others' lips with her fingers.

THE DEBATE OVER ORALISM

From the late 1800s to the 1970s, many schools forbade the use of sign language, requiring deaf students to learn to speak instead. According to Jack Gannon, special assistant to the president of Gallaudet University, a school for the deaf and hard of hearing, such restrictions made many deaf people feel "cheated out of a good education. . . . Cheated out of a good relationship with their own families . . . because they were restricted to only one method, oralism."[2]

Today, the debate over oralism continues. Those who oppose the method feel it robs deaf people of their own culture or makes them feel inferior. Supporters, however, contend oralism helps the deaf communicate and compete in a hearing world. Today, many deaf people learn to both sign and speak.

hear. In the spring of 1890, she began speech lessons with Sarah Fuller, principal of the Horace Mann School for the Deaf in Boston. For her lessons, Helen placed her fingers on Fuller's lips and in her mouth as Fuller spoke so that she could feel the correct positioning of the lips and tongue for each sound. By mimicking Fuller's movements, Helen learned to pronounce *m*, *p*, *a*, *s*, *t*, and *i* before the end of her first lesson. During the course of her speech lessons, Helen also learned to read lips by placing her fingers on a speaker's lips, nose, and throat. Helen's ability to lip-read meant even those who did not know the manual language could communicate with her.

After 11 speech lessons, Helen could say several words,

Sarah Fuller teaches a language class for elementary students in 1893.

though only her teachers and others who knew her well could understand her. Determined to improve, she practiced daily with Sullivan. Even though she still had a long way to go, Helen rejoiced in her new ability. "My thoughts used to beat against my finger tips like little birds striving to gain their freedom," she said, "until one day Miss Fuller opened wide the prison-door and let them escape."[3]

"The Frost King"

Helen was home in the fall of 1891 enjoying time with her family, which included new baby brother Phillips Brooks. She wrote a story called "The Frost King." The story was about fairies who left jars and vases with colored gems in the trees. The gems were melted by Mr. Sun, leaving the trees coated with the bright colors of fall. When she showed the story to her family members, they were amazed and asked where she had read it, but Helen replied that she had made the story up herself. She decided to send it to Anagnos as a birthday present.

Anagnos was so enchanted with the story that he had it printed in the Perkins alumni magazine. A copy also appeared in the *Goodson Gazette*, a newspaper published by the Virginia Institution for the Education of the Deaf and Dumb and of the Blind. *Dumb* used to mean "unable to speak." A reader of that paper soon pointed out, however, that Helen's story bore a striking resemblance to a story called "The Frost Fairies," which had been written by Margaret Canby and published in her book *Birdie and His Fairy Friends* in 1873. In some parts, the two stories matched word for word.

Embarrassed, Anagnos printed a retraction of the story and confronted Helen. The 11-year-old girl was devastated by the accusation of plagiarism. "It made us feel so bad to think that people thought we had been untrue and wicked," she wrote in her diary. "My heart was full of tears, for I love the beautiful truth with my whole heart and mind."[4] Helen insisted she had no memory of ever reading Canby's story, and Sullivan claimed she had never read the story to her student. As both Helen and Sullivan searched for answers, they discovered that Sophia Hopkins, with whom Helen had stayed during the summer of 1888, owned a copy of Canby's book. They thought perhaps Hopkins had read the book to Helen, who had forgotten about the story until she set out to write "The Frost King," not realizing the idea was not her own. Over the years, Helen's various biographers have disputed this story, saying that Sullivan likely did read the story to Helen but panicked and denied it when the plagiarism charges came up.

MARGARET CANBY AND "THE FROST KING"

As she dealt with the controversy surrounding her story "The Frost King," Helen received numerous letters of support, including one from Margaret Canby, the author whose story Helen was said to have plagiarized. Canby recognized that Helen's story was remarkably like her own and even pointed out several other of Helen's stories that included lines from her own works. But rather than accusing the child of plagiarism, she praised Helen's memory and concentration: "To have heard the story once, three years ago . . . and then to have been able to reproduce it so vividly, even adding some touches of her own in perfect keeping with the rest, which really improve the original, is something that very few girls of riper age, and with every advantage of sight, hearing, and even great talents for composition, could have done as well, if at all. Under the circumstances, I do not see how any one can be so unkind as to call it a plagiarism."[5]

Anagnos launched an official inquiry into the matter. He called both Helen and Sullivan to testify before a court of investigation made up of Perkins teachers and officers. As Helen waited for the court's verdict, she was distraught. "As I lay in my bed that night, I wept as I hope few children have wept," she later wrote. "I felt so cold, I imagined I should die before morning, and the thought comforted me."[6] Ultimately, four members of the court believed Helen had deliberately plagiarized the story; the other four took Helen's side. Anagnos was called on for the deciding vote, and he ruled that Helen was innocent of deliberate deception.

After "The Frost King" incident, Helen and Sullivan left the Perkins Institution for good. For years afterward, Helen lived in fear she would accidentally plagiarize someone else's words. She would stop in the middle of writing a letter or conversing with a friend and spell to her teacher, "I am not sure it is mine."[7]

To help Helen overcome her fears, Sullivan convinced her to write a story about her life for the *Youth's Companion* magazine. Although Helen did not enjoy writing about herself, people around the country responded to her article. She began receiving mail by the bagful—61 letters in one week alone.[8] She replied to as many as she could.

New Adventures

In 1888, Helen's father lost his position as a US marshal, leaving the family struggling for money. John S. Spaulding came to the rescue, offering to provide for Helen for life. He was an elderly businessman and philanthropist who gave money to causes to support the blind. With Spaulding's support, Helen and Sullivan traveled to Washington, DC, for the second inauguration of President Cleveland in March 1893. Afterward, they went to Niagara Falls in New York, where Helen felt the water "rushing and plunging with impetuous fury at my feet."[9]

That summer, Alexander Graham Bell escorted Helen and her teacher to the World's Columbian Exposition in Chicago, Illinois. Helen was allowed to touch all of the exhibits, including a diamond worth

HELPING OTHERS

In 1891, Helen's dog wandered away from home and was shot by a police officer. People from around the world wanted to send Helen money for a new dog. But she asked that the funds instead be used to send a young deaf-blind boy named Tommy Stringer to school. She sent letters to the editors of several newspapers, soliciting funds for Tommy as well. Ultimately, her efforts raised $1,600—enough to send Tommy to Perkins's kindergarten for the blind.[10]

$100,000. Her favorites were the bronze sculptures from France, which felt lifelike under her fingertips. During her three weeks at the fair, admiring crowds eager to catch a glimpse of her followed her around.

Back to Her Studies

Even as she traveled, Helen continued studying on her own, reading about Greek, Roman, and US history and teaching herself French. She also spent many hours practicing her speech with Sullivan. After the World's Columbian Exposition, Helen and Sullivan traveled to Pennsylvania, where Dr. John D. Irons tutored her in arithmetic, Latin, history, geography, and literature. Helen enjoyed her studies as much as ever. "I want to learn more and more about everything in this beautiful, wonderful world," she wrote. "Every day I find how little I know; for I catch glimpses on all sides of treasures of history, language, and science,—a beautiful world of knowledge,—and I long to see everything, know everything, and learn everything."[11]

In the summer of 1894, Helen and Sullivan traveled to Chautauqua, New York, for a meeting of the American Association to Promote the Teaching of Speech to the Deaf. There they met John D. Wright and

Helen's lifelong dedication to studying broadened her horizons.

Dr. Thomas Humason, who supported oralism and were opening a new school for the deaf in New York City. The focus of the school would be to teach speech to the deaf, and they thought they could help Helen learn to speak normally—and possibly even to sing. Helen could not wait to sign up.

Life in New York

Helen entered the Wright-Humason School for the Deaf in October 1894. The 14-year-old girl was the only deaf-blind student at the school, where she studied arithmetic, geography, literature, history, French, and German. She especially enjoyed her German lessons, since her German teacher knew the manual alphabet and could talk to her directly. Her other teachers had to talk to her through Sullivan.

The main focus of Helen's studies, though, was speech. She took lessons not only in pronunciation but also in tone and vocal quality. Helen put every effort into improving her voice. "How I should like to speak like other people!" she wrote. "I should be willing to work night and day if only it could be accomplished."[12] But her speech showed little improvement, and many people still struggled to understand her. Helen later said her greatest disappointment in life was her inability to speak clearly.

Helen's fame spread, and while in New York she met many influential people, whom she came to consider friends. Among them were writers such as Samuel Clemens (often known by his pen name, Mark Twain) and William Dean Howells; oil tycoons John

D. Rockefeller and Henry H. Rogers; and actors Joseph Jefferson and Sir Henry Irving.

Helen studied at Wright-Humason for two years. Shortly after she completed her studies there, in August 1896, her father died. This was Helen's first encounter with death, and she was heartbroken. "I never knew how dearly I loved my father until I realized that I had lost him," she wrote.[13]

For comfort, Helen turned to Swedenborgianism, a religion Bell's secretary John Hitz had recently introduced to her. Based on the teachings of eighteenth-century Swedish theologian Emanuel Swedenborg, the religion emphasized the importance of the soul over the body. Since the physical world was often remote to her senses, Swedenborg's focus on the spiritual world appealed to Helen.

THE REAL HELEN

In a paper written for the American Association to Promote the Teaching of Speech to the Deaf, Sullivan attempted to dispel the myths surrounding her student and point out what was truly extraordinary about her. She wrote that Helen's "'marvelous accomplishments' . . . consist only in her being able to speak and write . . . with greater ease and fluency than the average seeing and hearing child of her age. . . . Helen Keller is neither a 'phenomenal child,' 'an intellectual prodigy,' nor an 'extraordinary genius' but simply a very bright and lovely child, unmarred by self-consciousness or any taint of evil."[14]

CHAPTER
FIVE

HIGHER EDUCATION

Through all her years of study, the idea of attending college was always at the back of Keller's mind. Although few women attended college at the time—and no deaf-blind person had ever enrolled in an institution of higher education—Keller was determined to try. Her goal was to get into Radcliffe College, the women's affiliate of Harvard University (which accepted only men at the time). But first she needed to attend a school that could prepare her for the college entrance exams. She applied and was accepted to the Cambridge School for Young Ladies in Massachusetts.

Keller's benefactor, John S. Spaulding, had died in January 1896 and had not provided ongoing funding for Keller in his will. Without his support, Keller was not sure how she could afford to attend the Cambridge School. But her friend Samuel Clemens sent out appeals

With Sullivan by her side, Keller was determined to continue her education.

SAMUEL CLEMENS

Of all the influential people Keller met in her lifetime, Samuel Clemens was one of her favorites, and she remained close to him until his death. Keller especially loved Clemens because "he never made me feel that my opinions were worthless, as so many people do. He knew that we do not think with eyes and ears, and that our capacity for thought is not measured by five senses."[1] Clemens, in return, said Keller was the most remarkable woman he had ever met.

to several wealthy friends, convincing them to fund Keller's education.

Keller entered the Cambridge School on October 1, 1896. All of her 100 classmates could both see and hear. Although a few of the girls learned the manual alphabet and Keller sometimes joined in their games, she often felt isolated.

Because the Cambridge School was not set up for people with disabilities, none of Keller's teachers had experience teaching the deaf or blind, and only a few learned the manual language. Sullivan attended all of Keller's classes with her and spelled the teachers' lectures into her hand. Since Keller's books were not available in embossed print or braille, Sullivan had to spell those to her, too.

By the end of her first year, Keller was ready to take a portion of her college entrance exams. Sullivan was not allowed to accompany Keller to the tests so there

Some of the books Helen used to study were embossed with raised type.

would be no suspicion of cheating. Instead, Arthur Gilman, the school's director, spelled the test questions to Keller, who typed her answers. That year, Keller took exams in elementary and advanced German, French, Latin, English, and Greek and Roman history. She passed every exam and earned honors in English and German. Gilman was impressed, writing, "I think that I may say that no candidate in Harvard or Radcliffe College was graded higher than Keller in English. . . . No man or woman has ever in my experience got ready for these examinations in so brief a time."[2]

Almost Separated

The next fall, Keller resumed her studies at the Cambridge School, this time with a heavy emphasis on mathematical subjects such as physics, algebra, and geometry, in addition to astronomy, Latin, and Greek. But her embossed math textbooks were not yet ready, and she had not yet received a braille typewriter for working out math problems in class. She struggled to keep up. When Keller missed a few days of school in November, Gilman accused Sullivan of overworking her. He reduced Keller's course load, cutting out geometry and astronomy. A humiliated Keller felt "as if I had been cheated out of my proper share in the school work."[3]

Gilman also contacted Kate Keller and told her that they should find a replacement for Sullivan, who he felt was "better adapted to the training of a girl in the beginning than of a young lady who has already far outstripped her."[4] When Sullivan learned of this, she warned Keller the two might soon be separated. Keller was distraught. She sobbed desperately, refusing to eat or sleep until her friend Joseph Edgar Chamberlin arrived to take her from the school to his house in Wrentham, Massachusetts. There he told her she might have to decide between her mother and her teacher. "If I have to decide between my mother and Teacher," she replied, "I will stay with Teacher."[5]

But Keller did not have to choose. Her mother decided not to replace Sullivan after all, and she pulled Keller out of the Cambridge School. Sullivan and Keller remained at Chamberlin's house, where a tutor named Merton Keith visited once a week to continue Keller's preparation for the Radcliffe entrance exams. Keith focused especially on algebra and geometry, Keller's weakest subjects. In October 1898, Keller and Sullivan moved to Boston, where Keith began giving Keller daily

A BRAILLE TEST

Only two days before Keller was scheduled to take her college entrance exams, she learned the tests had been copied for her into American braille—one of five different braille systems. Although Keller was familiar with this form of braille, she had used only English braille for her mathematical studies. Because the mathematical symbols in the two systems differed greatly, Keller spent the next two days feverishly studying American braille. When test day came, she struggled through the math portions but managed to pass. She later became involved in the movement to develop a single, standardized braille system. "A plague on all these points," she wrote in 1907, referring to the varying systems of raised dots. "Let us have one system, whether it is an ideal one or not."[6] Her desire for a single system was met in 1932 with the development of Standard English Braille.

Radcliffe College, approximately a decade after Keller arrived in 1900

lessons. By June 1899, Keller was ready to take her entrance exams. She passed them all.

College Student

Although Keller could have entered Radcliffe in the fall of 1899, she decided to spend another year studying English literature, French, German, and Latin with Keith. She wanted to be thoroughly prepared in each of these subjects, since she knew the professors at Radcliffe would make no special exceptions for her circumstances.

In fact, Radcliffe had not really wanted to admit Keller at all. As Radcliffe's dean, Agnes Irwin, later said, "Radcliffe did not desire Helen Keller as a student. It was necessary that all instruction should reach her through Miss Sullivan, and this necessity presented difficulties."[7] Radcliffe's resistance only spurred Keller on. "They didn't want me at Radcliffe, and, being stubborn, I chose

to override their objections," she later told President Woodrow Wilson.[8]

Keller entered Radcliffe in the fall of 1900. As at the Cambridge School, Keller often found herself lonely in the world of hearing and sighted students. But she had little time to notice her isolation as she focused on her studies. Once again, Sullivan had to spell every lecture into Keller's hand, since only one of Keller's teachers learned the manual language. Each night, Sullivan spent five or more hours spelling Keller's textbooks to her. The task put a severe strain on Sullivan's eyes, and doctors warned that only complete rest would keep her from losing her sight. Worried about her teacher's eyes, Keller would often pretend she had understood her lessons so that Sullivan would not have to reread them. As Keller struggled to keep up, she longed for time to reflect on what she was learning. "I used to have time to think, to reflect, my mind and I. . . . But in college there is no time to commune with one's thoughts," she said.[9]

At Radcliffe, Keller studied French, German, English composition, government, economics, history, Shakespeare, literature, and philosophy. She particularly excelled in a composition course taught by Dr. Charles T. Copeland, who encouraged Keller to write from her own perspective, opening up new possibilities to the young woman. "I have always accepted other people's experiences and observations as a matter of course," she wrote to Copeland. "It never occurred to me that it might be worthwhile to make my own observations and describe the experiences peculiarly my own. . . . Henceforth I am resolved to be myself, to live my own life, and write my own thoughts when I have any."[10]

The Story of My Life

During Keller's second year at Radcliffe, she was asked by the editors of the *Ladies Home Journal* magazine to write an autobiography in a series of five monthly installments. It was a time-consuming task, as Keller had to type each page on a typewriter—since that was the form it would have to be in for publication—and

Keller would be a famous writer for her entire adult life.

then have it read back to her so she could make changes and corrections.

As Keller struggled to complete her draft, a friend introduced her to John Macy, a 25-year-old English instructor at Harvard. Macy quickly learned the manual alphabet and began helping Keller edit her story, which was also published as a book called *The Story of My Life* in 1903. The book won wide critical acclaim, but sales were slow, with only 10,000 copies sold in the first two years.[11] Over time, however, *The Story of My Life* became a classic. It has been translated into 50 languages and remains in print today. In 1996, the New York Public Library named it one of the 100 most important books of the 1900s.

THE REAL GENIUS

Because of her lack of sight and hearing, some people doubted Keller really accomplished all that was credited to her. When she entered Radcliffe, rumors flew that Sullivan would be doing all the work for her. "Why don't they say outright that Miss Sullivan is entering Radcliffe instead of Helen Keller, a blind, deaf and dumb girl," some people said.[12] Because of these rumors, Sullivan was kept out of the examination room whenever Keller took a test, and records of Keller's exam results were kept on file in the dean's office. Many people asked to see them—they wanted proof that Keller was able to pass a test without Sullivan at her side.

Later, critics contended that Macy was the true author of *The Story of My Life* and that Sullivan wrote many of Keller's articles and speeches. Such rumors were put to rest when Keller continued turning out well-written books and articles even after Sullivan's and Macy's deaths.

Despite the book's wide praise, there were detractors as well. Critics especially protested Keller's use of visual and auditory descriptions, saying she could not possibly have seen or heard the things she wrote about. She responded that she had learned to use such expressions in order to communicate with people who could see and hear.

College Graduate

With her autobiography complete, Keller returned her focus to her studies. She was now aided by Sullivan as well as Macy, who pitched in to read to her whenever he could to spare Sullivan's eyesight.

On June 28, 1904, Keller and 95 other women graduated from Radcliffe College.

Keller was proud to be the first deaf-blind person to graduate from college.

Although newspapers reported that large crowds had gathered for the event, only a few close friends were there to cheer on Keller. Even her mother could not make it to the ceremony due to illness. Although Keller was disappointed by her mother's absence, she was more disappointed that Sullivan—who had attended all the same classes and read the same books—received no recognition during the ceremony.

Still, Keller was thrilled to earn her bachelor of arts degree, with the distinction of cum laude, or with honors. Afterward, she and Sullivan quietly slipped out of the celebration. It was time to start their new life.

CHAPTER
SIX

HAPPIEST YEARS

Only hours after Keller's graduation ceremony, she and Sullivan arrived at their new home, a large, old farmhouse they had purchased in Wrentham. There, Keller pondered what to do with the education she had worked so hard to achieve. She knew she wanted to work for the blind, but she was not yet sure how she could best assist them.

In the meantime, she and Sullivan settled into a quiet life. Each day, Keller got up at 6:00 a.m., dressed, styled her hair, and cleaned her room. Then she made the beds and set the table. She picked flowers to decorate the house and helped Sullivan with the dishes.

Macy often came to visit the two women, and he soon proposed to Sullivan. The two were married in early May 1905, as a friend spelled the words of the ceremony into Keller's hand. After the wedding, Macy moved into the house at Wrentham with Sullivan and Keller.

Sullivan remained Keller's eyes and ears as Keller moved into her adult life.

Keller later considered her days at Wrentham with Macy and Sullivan the happiest of her life. Macy strung a rope across a field so that Keller could take a quarter-mile (0.4 km) walk by herself. Both he and Sullivan dedicated themselves to keeping Keller intellectually stimulated, talking with her about what was going on in the news, literature, and science. The trio frequently entertained visitors, among them some of the top scholars of the day, who were always bringing talk of art, philosophy, literature, and politics.

A WORLD OF INTERESTS

Throughout her life, Keller found time to pursue numerous hobbies. She particularly enjoyed outdoor activities and from an early age learned to row. Although she usually took a companion along to control the rudder when she went out in her boat, she sometimes went alone and steered by the scent of the water grasses and lilies. She also swam, tying a rope from the shore around her waist so she would not go out too far.

On land, she loved to take walks or ride her tandem bicycle with a partner. She was an accomplished horsewoman and could even ride at a gallop as long as she was alongside another rider going the same pace.

Indoors, Keller enjoyed knitting, reading, and playing games. Among her favorites were checkers and chess, for which she had a special board and pieces that were sized or shaped differently so that she could distinguish between her pieces and those of her opponent. She also played solitaire with cards marked with braille numbers.

Keller enjoyed many outdoor activities, including horseback riding.

The World I Live In

Keller continued writing while at Wrentham, with Macy acting as her editor. In addition to articles for various magazines, she began work on a new book that would be called *The World I Live In*. Although she usually found writing a slow and agonizing process, she enjoyed working on this book, in which she discussed her unique sensory experience of the world. She explained that for her, the senses of touch and smell were adequate and she rarely felt disabled, despite the fact that she could not see or hear. "My hand is to me what your hearing and sight together are to you," she wrote.[1]

The World I Live In was published in 1908 and quickly became a critical success. Even as Keller continued writing about herself, however, she longed to pen works on other topics close to her heart, such as politics. But she found editors were not interested in her views about these subjects. "When I write seriously about the

DARKNESS NOT TERRIBLE

Although people often picture blindness as a state of horrible darkness, Keller wrote in *The World I Live In*, "To the blind child the dark is kindly. In it he finds nothing extraordinary or terrible. It is his familiar world."[2] Earlier, in *The Story of My Life*, she had compared blindness to being in a fog of "tangible white darkness."[3]

broader aspects of human life, people are apt to laugh and tell me that I know nothing about the practical world," she wrote.[4]

Even so, after *The World I Live In*, Keller began work on another book, called *The Song of the Stone Wall*. This epic poem about her exuberance in helping to rebuild a stone wall around her home was published in 1910.

Socialism

Keller had always been interested in politics, and in 1908, she read H. G. Wells's *New Worlds for Old*. The book lays out the case for socialism, a political system that emphasizes shared ownership and equality and holds that the government should take care of those in need. The book struck a chord with the young woman, who had always been appalled by injustice and poverty. She began reading everything she could about socialism, and in 1909, she became a member of the Socialist Party. Two years later, she joined the Industrial Workers of the World, a more militant socialist group, and declared she was committed to a socialist revolution. She supported labor strikes and blamed capitalism for most of the world's problems, including poverty, blindness, and deafness. In 1913, she published *Out of the Dark*, a series of essays explaining her socialist views. In it, she wrote of how the cause of the blind was connected to the cause of the poor around the world:

> We can subsidize [pay for] the work of the sightless; we can build special institutions and factories for them, and solicit the help of wealthy patrons. But the blind man cannot become an independent, self-supporting member of society . . . until all his seeing brothers have opportunity to work to the full extent of their ability. We know now that the welfare of the whole people is essential to the welfare of each.[5]

Keller's admirers were taken aback by her public support of such a radical cause. Although she had once been hailed as an angelic little girl who had conquered overwhelming odds, she was now denounced on the front pages of newspapers as a dangerous revolutionary. She did not mind. She was glad that for once the attention she received had nothing to do with her lack of sight and hearing.

But even as people denounced Keller's views, they also made excuses for her. Some said she was being exploited by Macy and Sullivan. But Sullivan was not a socialist, and Keller resented the implication she was simply parroting Macy's socialist views, as if she could not think for herself because she had disabilities. Some

The Industrial Workers of the World (IWW) organized the working class to try to overthrow the capitalist system.

critics went so far as to say Keller could not possibly know about the world of politics because she was deaf and blind. To this Keller responded, "I plead guilty to the charge that I am deaf and blind, though I forget the fact most of the time. . . . I have the advantage of a mind trained to think, and that is the difference between myself and most people, not my blindness and their sight."[6]

Despite the negative publicity, Keller continued speaking out for socialism. As the nation prepared for World War I (1914–1918), she also denounced the conflict. "I am opposed to all wars except those that are really fought for freedom," she wrote in a letter.[7] She called on workers to form a worldwide union and revolt against military service, actions that could lead to a person being arrested. "Let no working men join this army which Congress is trying to build up," she said. "I look upon the world as my fatherland, and every war has for me the horror of a family feud."[8] Keller also spoke out in favor of women's voting rights and birth control and campaigned against child labor and capital punishment.

Work for the Blind

Even as she embraced new causes, Keller remained committed to working for the blind. She wrote and spoke about the prevention of blindness caused by the disease ophthalmia neonatorum, which affects newborn babies. Although the disease is easily preventable if medicated eyedrops are given to newborn children, it had never before been publicly discussed because it was caused by a sexually transmitted infection in the mother. It was not considered respectable to discuss these issues.

In addition, Helen campaigned for job training for the blind so they could become useful members of society. "No anguish is keener than the sense of helplessness and self-condemnation which overwhelms them when they find every avenue to activity and usefulness closed to them," she said.[9] She frequently appeared before state legislatures to promote the cause of the blind as well.

A WISH TO SEE

Keller once wrote an article describing what she would wish to see if she were granted three days of sight. Among the first things she would look at, she said, were the faces of her teacher and her dogs. She wanted to see printed books, a baby, and the great museums of New York. She wanted to watch a Shakespearean play or see a movie. She would watch a sunrise, take a walk among the beauties of nature, and look out on the view from the top of the Empire State Building.

CHAPTER
SEVEN

LECTURES AND LOVE

From 1910 to 1913, Keller took voice lessons with Charles White, a singing teacher at the Boston Conservatory of Music. White concentrated on developing Keller's vocal chords and improving her ability to speak with rhythm and pitch so that she would sound less tinny and robotic. Although her speech never became perfect, it improved enough that she was often able to speak without an interpreter.

One of the main reasons Keller wanted to improve her voice was so she could take to the lecture circuit to earn money to provide for herself. In 1913, Keller and Sullivan made their debut on the lecture stage in Montclair, New Jersey. Although Keller felt as though her voice was out of control during the lecture, the crowd loved her, and the speech launched a 50-year career on the stage.

Keller, *left*, speaks on a stage with Sullivan assisting in 1919.

At first, Keller and Sullivan lectured close to home—in New York, New Jersey, and other locations on the East Coast. But soon they were traveling across the country and into Canada. They attracted huge audiences wherever they went, and powerful people such as inventor Thomas Edison and industrialist Henry Ford were among their admirers.

For each lecture, Sullivan took to the stage first, speaking about Keller's education. Then Keller joined her onstage and delivered a "Message of Happiness," encouraging the audience to be cheerful and do good works. Afterward, Keller answered the audience's questions. Although the audience often struggled to follow her coarse, high-pitched voice, they always went away moved by the experience.

GLASS EYES

Although Keller's right eye appeared normal, her left eye was disfigured and protruded slightly from her face. For that reason, she had always been photographed from the right. But before she began to tour on the lecture circuit, she decided to have both eyes surgically removed and replaced with glass ones. Afterward, many people took notice of Keller's beautiful blue eyes. Few realized they were not real eyes.

Accepting Help

In 1913, while Keller and Sullivan were in Maine for a lecture, Sullivan suddenly collapsed with the flu. Keller was alone with her teacher at the time and had no way to call for help. After a while, Sullivan felt well enough to call a doctor herself, and the two were soon on their way home. But the scare made Keller realize she needed more help.

A few years earlier, wealthy industrialist Andrew Carnegie had offered to provide Keller with a pension of $5,000 a year.[1] Keller had graciously declined his offer, telling him, "I hope to enlarge my life and work by my own efforts."[2] As a socialist, she did not feel she could in good conscience take money from an industrialist. Now, however, Keller contacted Carnegie to accept his help. The income he provided, along with funds from other friends and the fees earned on lecture tours, allowed Keller to feel more financially stable.

In addition to accepting financial help, in 1914, Keller and Sullivan also hired a new assistant, Polly Thomson. Although Thomson had never heard of Keller and Sullivan before joining them, she soon became indispensable. She learned the manual language, kept track of expenses, mapped tour routes, and managed the household.

Meanwhile, Macy felt neglected as Sullivan continued dedicating herself to Keller. He moved out

Thomson, *left*, became Keller's devoted long-term companion.

of the house in Wrentham the three had shared. Keller tried to reconcile the couple, but her efforts proved fruitless. Although they never divorced, their marriage was in effect over by 1914. Keller spent hours during lecture tours comforting her teacher. She, too, grieved the loss of a friend who had broadened her world.

A Love of Her Own

By the time she entered the lecture circuit, Keller was 33 years old, and she had no thoughts of ever marrying. When she was younger, her mother had forbidden her from dating, in part because society of that time frowned on the idea of people with disabilities marrying. Many people feared that if those who were disabled married, they would produce more children with disabilities. An entire movement, called eugenics, was built around the idea of preventing such people from having children.

For her part, Keller believed, "It would be a severe handicap to any man to saddle upon him the dead weight of my infirmities. I know I have nothing to give a man that would make up for such an unnatural burden."[3] Although Keller sometimes thought of love, she said it was "like a beautiful flower which I may not touch, but whose fragrance makes the garden a place of delight just the same."[4]

EUGENICS IN AMERICA

Throughout the late 1800s and early 1900s, the eugenics movement flourished in the United States and Europe. The goal of the movement was to improve the human race by eliminating anyone who was considered "socially unfit."[5] This included the poor, criminals, and those with disabilities such as epilepsy, blindness, or deafness, among others. Supporters of eugenics fought to prevent such people from marrying. In addition, thousands of "unfit" people were involuntarily sterilized. Eugenics fell out of favor after World War II (1939–1945), when German dictator Adolf Hitler used it to justify the extermination of millions of Jews.

But in the fall of 1916, Keller's resolve not to marry was tested. Peter Fagan had recently been hired as a secretary to take care of Keller's correspondence. One night, the young man came into her study. He began spelling words of love into her hand, promising that if she would marry him, he would read to her and take care of her. Keller was surprised by Fagan's declaration of love, but she did not find it unwelcome, and she agreed to marry him.

Because Fagan knew Keller's mother would not approve of the marriage, he convinced Keller to keep their engagement a secret. Keller reluctantly agreed. But when a newspaper story announced the two had applied for a marriage license, the secret was out. Keller's mother, who was visiting, demanded that Fagan leave and forced her 36-year-old daughter to print a public denial of the engagement.

Keller and Fagan did not give up. First they made plans to meet on the boat Keller was to take to Alabama to visit her sister, Mildred. But Keller's mother again discovered their plans and took Keller to Alabama by train instead. Persevering, Fagan traveled to Mildred's house in Alabama. But Mildred's husband ran him off with a gun. A few nights later, Mildred heard a sound on the porch. It was Keller, waiting with her bags packed for Fagan. He never showed up—or if he did, he sensed trouble and left—and Keller did not hear from him again.

After, Keller did not blame her family for preventing her from marrying. Instead, she thought she had been foolish to fall in love. But she always cherished the memory of that love, writing that it would "remain in my life, a little island of joy surrounded by dark waters. I am glad that I have had the experience of being loved and desired."[6]

On Her Own

In the midst of the drama with Fagan, Keller had been left without her teacher as Sullivan had traveled first to

SOUNDING THE ALARM

While Keller was staying at the home of her sister, Mildred, in Alabama, her sense of smell saved the family from disaster. One night, while she was lying in bed, she noticed a strange scent, but since it was similar to the odor of steam in the kitchen pipes, she did not worry about it. A short time later, she thought she smelled smoke from outside. Again, she was unconcerned. But then she smelled tar and burning wood. Suddenly, she realized the house was on fire. She ran to alert her mother. The family was saved, and the fire department arrived to put out the fire, which had started under Keller's bed as a result of a faulty chimney.

Although Keller was instrumental in sounding the alarm, she was upset she had not been able to warn her family sooner. "It distresses me to think that my lack of sight might have proved fatal to my loved ones," she wrote to Sullivan. "It seems as if I could never sleep quietly here again without putting my face down close to the floor and hunting all over for an odor or a hidden spark."[7]

Keller hated being separated from her teacher.

Lake Placid, New York, and then to Puerto Rico to recover from tuberculosis. Happily, she later discovered she had never had the disease; her records had been mixed up with those of another patient. During the five months Sullivan was gone, Keller stayed with her family, struggling against feelings of isolation and boredom. She was reminded once again of just how much she needed her teacher. "I saw more clearly than ever before how inseparably our lives were bound together. How lonely and bleak the world would be without her," she said.[8]

When Sullivan finally returned, she and Keller sold their home in Wrentham and moved to Forest Hills, just outside New York City. There, Keller jumped back into the political scene and again voiced her support of the socialist cause.

A MEDAL FOR SULLIVAN

In 1915, San Francisco, California, hosted a Helen Keller Day, at which Sullivan was honored with a Teacher's Medal. Keller rejoiced more in the honor given to her teacher than in all those she had received herself. She said, "She could have lived her own life. . . . She has given me the best years of her womanhood, and you see her still giving herself to me day by day."[9]

CHAPTER
EIGHT

STAGE AND SCREEN

Although Sullivan did not have tuberculosis, she was ill—too ill to lecture. And even if she had been well, the demand for lectures had dried up with the United States' entry into World War I in April 1917. So when an opportunity to create a movie of Keller's life came up in 1918, Keller jumped at it. She was determined to save money to provide for Sullivan in case of her own death. In addition, she thought a movie would give her an opportunity to carry her message of courage and happiness to the world.

Keller, Sullivan, and Thomson traveled to Hollywood for the filming of the movie, which would be called *Deliverance*. Keller played herself in the movie's later scenes, responding to the director's cues, which were conveyed through stomps on the floor. When they were not filming, Keller, Sullivan, and Thomson enjoyed meeting some of the top stars of the day, including comedic actor Charlie Chaplin.

Keller enjoyed a long and successful stage career.

By December 1918, filming was finished. But Keller and her friends were not happy with the results. In an attempt to make the movie a commercial hit, the studio had included numerous fanciful scenes that had nothing to do with Keller's life. A few changes were made, but Keller was still disappointed with the film.

Taking to Vaudeville

Although *Deliverance* received positive reviews from critics, it did not do well at the box office. Still needing money, Keller came up with a new plan. She and Sullivan would perform on the vaudeville stage.

Beginning in 1920, Keller and Sullivan traveled the country as a vaudeville act, often performing before standing-room-only crowds. Keller loved vaudeville. The work was easier than lecturing, as she and Sullivan gave two 20-minute performances a day in place of an hour-and-a-half-long lecture. And they stayed in one location for an entire week rather than packing up and

Not One Dissenting Voice Among the New York Critics

Mr George Kleine PRESENTS
The 8th Wonder of the World
HELEN
KELLER
in the Photo Play Beautiful
DELIVERANCE
DIRECT FROM HER GREAT TRIUMPH
AT THE LYRIC THEATRE
NEW YORK CITY

Directed By GEORGE FOSTER PLATT

Deliverance sought to provide hope and inspiration, but its imaginary scenes and heavy symbolism got in the way of telling Keller's story.

moving after a single show. Vaudeville even paid much better. They earned up to $2,000 a week, compared with the $300 they had earned for each lecture.[1] Plus, vaudeville was fun. "I found the world of vaudeville much more amusing than the world I had always lived in, and I liked it. I liked to feel the warm tide of human life pulsing round and round me," she wrote.[2]

As in their lecture tours, Sullivan (and later, Thomson) took the stage first and described Keller's education. Then Keller entered and told the audience she could feel their applause with her feet. She gave a short speech, telling the audience, "I was dumb; now I speak. I owe this to the hands and hearts of others. Through their love I found my soul and God and happiness. . . . Alone we can do so little. Together we can do so much."[3] Afterward, Keller answered questions. She was often asked about her political views. She did not hide her continuing commitment to socialism.

Keller faced one of her greatest challenges on the vaudeville stage in 1921. When she was in Los Angeles, California, she received word her mother had died. Although Keller always thought her mother blamed her illness for destroying the family's happiness, the two had grown closer in recent years. Now, Keller had only two hours to deal with her grief before she had to perform. When she went onstage, she managed to keep the audience from suspecting anything was wrong.

Life's Work

By 1923, Keller had performed across the country. But demand for her act was falling off, since there was no way to make it fresh. Once again, she was in need of money. That year, Moses Charles Migel, director of the newly formed American Foundation for the Blind (AFB), requested Keller's help in raising funds for the

Her work educating and fund-raising for the blind around the world remained important to Keller for the rest of her life.

organization. Although as a socialist Keller opposed philanthropy from the wealthy, she agreed to take the job, saying, "It is not pleasant to go begging even for the best of causes, but in our present civilization most philanthropic and educational institutions are supported by public donations and gifts from wealthy citizens. This is a wretched way, but we have not yet learned a better one."[4] The AFB agreed to pay Keller and Sullivan $2,000 a month to speak at four meetings a week.[5]

At first, Keller and Sullivan held fund-raising meetings at the homes of wealthy individuals. But so many people wanted to hear them speak they soon moved their events to larger venues such as churches. Keller and Sullivan quickly adapted their vaudeville performance for the fund-raising meetings. First, Sullivan would talk about Keller's education, and then Keller would make a short speech, answer questions, and request donations for the AFB.

Within three years, Keller, Sullivan, and Thomson had crisscrossed the country, holding 249 meetings in 123 cities. They had addressed 250,000 people.[6] In some cities, they were disappointed with the amount raised. But in others they had great success. In Philadelphia, Pennsylvania, they raised $21,000 in one afternoon.[7]

In addition to raising funds, Keller became a tireless lobbyist for the AFB. Her efforts led Congress to adopt the Pratt-Smoot Bill in 1931, establishing the National Library Service for the Blind and Physically Handicapped. Keller was also instrumental in efforts to create a standardized system of braille. In addition, she petitioned state legislatures to set up committees for assistance for the blind and to fund blind education.

Keller remained associated with the AFB for the rest of her life. At the AFB's request, she distanced herself from the socialist movement, rarely speaking publicly about socialism after 1922. Privately, however, she remained loyal to the cause.

Midstream

In 1927, Keller took a leave of absence from fund-raising for the AFB to continue her autobiography. When she sat down to write, though, she found she dreaded the task. So when she was asked to write a book about Emanuel Swedenborg, she eagerly worked on that instead. The result was *My Religion*, which was published in 1927 and soon became a text widely used among Swedenborg's followers.

HONORS AND AWARDS

In her lifetime, Keller received honorary degrees from Temple University in Philadelphia, Scotland's University of Glasgow, South Africa's University of the Witwatersrand, and Harvard. In 1964, she was presented with the Presidential Medal of Freedom, the highest civilian award in the United States. The next year, she was elected into the Women's Hall of Fame at the New York World's Fair. And in 1973, she was inducted into the National Women's Hall of Fame.

After she finished *My Religion*, Keller turned back to her autobiography. She had years' worth of notes to go through. Sullivan and Thomson helped her, as did Nella Braddy Henney, an editorial assistant from Keller's publisher, Doubleday, who soon became a close friend.

When *Midstream* was published in 1929, most reviewers gave it high praise. But some brought up the old criticism that Keller described sights and sounds of which she could have no firsthand knowledge.

Good-Bye, Teacher

Keller resumed her busy pace of fund-raising and lobbying for the AFB. By this time, Sullivan's eyesight was failing. Keller did what she could to comfort her teacher. She understood blindness would be harder for Sullivan than it was for her. "All my life I have lived in a dark and silent world. I seldom think of my limitations,

COLOR ASSOCIATIONS

One of the biggest complaints of those who criticized *Midstream* was Keller's use of color. She described, for example, blue, yellow, and red flowers and a "white hilltop fading into the purple distance."[8] She wrote of how "the shoulder of the moon turned pink as she threw a scarlet scarf over her head."[9] Critics of such language contended that though Keller used her hands to sense the world around her, color was not something that could be learned through touch.

But Keller explained that, for her, each color conjured up not a visual image but an association. Pink was like a baby's cheek, while gray was like a soft shawl, and lilac brought to mind the faces of people she loved. She said there were two kinds of brown: a warm, friendly brown, like that of the earth, and a worn, tired brown like the trunk of a tree or wrinkled hands. When she thought of a color that sparkled, she imagined soap bubbles in her hands.

and they never make me sad, but to see the light failing in another's eye is terrible, especially when one is unable to do anything about the tragedy," she said.[10] To provide Sullivan with needed rest, Keller and Thomson took her to Scotland in 1930.

In April 1931, Keller helped organize the first-ever World Council for the Blind, which brought together delegates from 32 countries. During the course of the conference, Keller was constantly on the move, entertaining the delegates at lunches and dinners and arranging a reception at the White House.

After the conference, Keller, Sullivan, and Thomson traveled to France and Yugoslavia. And in 1932, they returned to Scotland, where Keller received an honorary doctor of law degree from the University of Glasgow. Keller spent much of the trip writing magazine articles, delivering speeches, and visiting schools. She took time out to attend a garden party at Buckingham Palace in London, England, where King George and Queen Mary marveled over her ability to communicate.

In the summer of 1936, Sullivan suffered a heart attack and was rushed to the hospital. Although she came home afterward, she never fully recovered. On October 20, she died with Keller sitting at her side.

CHAPTER
NINE

LATER YEARS

Keller was 56 years old when Sullivan died. She and her teacher had been together for nearly 50 years. Now, Keller was not sure how to go on without her. "The anguish which makes me feel cut in two prevents me from writing another word about these life-wrecking changes," she wrote in a journal begun shortly after Sullivan's death and published in 1938.[1]

In an effort to escape the painful memories that surrounded them at home, Keller and Thomson sailed for Scotland two days after Sullivan's funeral. Keller used the time to grieve. She also answered the hundreds of sympathy letters she had received. By early February 1937, Keller was ready to return home. Because Keller could not live alone, Thomson became her new constant companion. Although Keller never loved Thomson as she had loved Sullivan, the two still became close.

Soon after her return to the United States, Keller was appointed Counselor of the Bureau of National and International Relations for the AFB, a position that

Keller and Thomson traveled widely after Sullivan's death.

involved traveling around the world in support of the blind. In 1937, she and Thomson traveled to Japan to raise money for the blind and deaf there. As they toured the country delivering nearly 100 lectures, they were treated as celebrities. Schoolchildren waving Japanese and American flags shouted Keller's name and threw flowers in her path. She met nearly every high-level Japanese official and was even received by the emperor and empress, a privilege rarely granted foreigners.

After returning to the United States, Keller and Thomson sold the home in Forest Hills—which had too many memories of Sullivan—and moved to Westport, Connecticut. A trustee of the AFB built them a new home, which Keller named Arcan Ridge. Keller could walk around the property alone, and she got up at 5:00 a.m. every summer morning to tend the home's many gardens and paths.

"The Crowning Experience of My Life"

After the United States entered World War II (1939–1945) in 1941, Keller began visiting military hospitals to offer encouragement to soldiers who had been blinded in the war. She spoke with the soldiers realistically about their new life, telling them that once they learned to cope with their blindness, they could enjoy a full life, with friends, family, and accomplishments of their own. She was living proof it could be done.

As Keller held their hands or kissed their heads, the soldiers were inspired and comforted. "You are the most impressive and stimulating visitor we have had at

CONTINUING KELLER'S WORK

Today, many organizations are working to continue Keller's mission:

- The American Foundation for the Overseas Blind, a sister organization of the AFB, is today known as Helen Keller International. Its current mission centers on preventing blindness and reducing malnutrition around the world.

- The American Foundation for the Blind continues to operate as well. Today, the AFB helps the blind find job opportunities, provides new technologies to aid the blind in their day-to-day lives, and lobbies for legislation to improve their lives.

- In 1925, the International Convention of the Lions Clubs accepted a challenge from Keller to be "Knights of the Blind in this crusade against darkness."[2] Today, Lions Clubs continue to support programs aimed at preventing blindness, restoring sight, and improving eye health.

- The Helen Keller Foundation was established in 1988 to focus on research and education related to blindness and deafness. The foundation has since developed new surgical techniques, identified new ways to prevent blindness, and provided educational programs to more than 500,000 students.

our hospitals," a general wrote her, "and that puts you ahead of the Hollywood blondes [and] brunettes."[3] In six months, Keller toured 70 military hospitals across the country.[4] She later called the work "the crowning experience of my life."[5]

World Traveler

In 1946, a year after World War II ended, Keller and Thomson flew to Europe, where they offered comfort to people there who were blinded in the war. While they were in Europe, they learned their house had burned down due to a furnace malfunction. Nearly all of Keller's braille books had been lost in the fire, as had the nearly complete manuscript of the biography she was writing about Sullivan. But after the suffering and devastation Keller and Thomson had seen in war-ravaged Europe, they felt their own troubles were minor and said they would simply rebuild.

The tour of Europe was the first Keller made for the American Foundation for the Overseas Blind (AFOB), a sister organization of the AFB. Over the next 11 years, she would visit 35 countries in Asia, Africa, and South America on behalf of the AFOB.[6] The US State Department would come to regard her as its

Eleanor Roosevelt, *left*, and Keller attended a reception in Keller's honor in 1936, while Roosevelt was still the First Lady.

second-most persuasive ambassador spreading goodwill abroad, after former First Lady Eleanor Roosevelt.

After traveling to South Africa in 1951 and Latin America in 1953, Keller decided it was time to start again on her biography of Sullivan. She spent long days at her desk, reliving the past and pouring it onto the page. The work was physically and emotionally grueling. Keller's fingers were not as sensitive as they had once been, and she had difficulty reading her braille notes. At times, she broke down in tears as she remembered her teacher and realized what Sullivan had given up for her.

When *Teacher* was published in 1955, readers remarked on its emotional intensity.

By the time *Teacher* hit the shelves, Keller was 75 years old. But she was not ready to retire from her work for the blind. She set out on one of her longest trips, covering 40,000 miles (64,000 km) in five months as she reviewed the living conditions of people with disabilities in India, Hong Kong, the Philippines, and Japan.[7]

DOCUMENTARY BIOGRAPHY

In the midst of her overseas travels, Keller remained at home long enough to work on a documentary about her life, *The Unconquered*. For the film, Keller was followed nearly everywhere by cameras and even joined in a dance specially choreographed for her by famed dancer Martha Graham. Completed in 1953, the film earned critical acclaim and won an Academy Award for best feature-length documentary.

Keller returned home to receive an honorary degree from Harvard—the first the university had ever awarded a woman. In the spring of 1957, she embarked on her last tour on behalf of the AFOB, this time journeying to Scandinavia. But Keller was not planning to take it easy. The 77-year-old told her friends, "I shall devote my old age to study," and she spent her days reading foreign languages, history, philosophy, and poetry.[8]

Another Good-Bye

Even as Keller and Thomson made their last world tours, Thomson's health was failing. Even so, she became possessive of Keller and refused to let others spell to Keller unless she was with them. She resisted training anyone to take her place.

In 1957, Thomson suffered a stroke. The next year, she experienced several seizures. Thomson died on March 21, 1960. She had been with Keller for 46 years.

A MONUMENT TO KELLER

In October 2009, a statue of Keller at the water pump was unveiled at the US Capitol in Washington, DC. The state of Alabama commissioned the statue as part of the National Statuary Hall Collection, in which each state displays two statues. The statue of Keller is the only one of a child and the first of a person with disabilities. Former Alabama governor Bob Riley said the statue would catch the eyes of the millions of children who tour the Capitol, reminding them "that courage and strength can exist in the most unlikely places."[9]

To the End

During Thomson's last years, Winifred Corbally and Evelyn Seide had been brought in to help run Keller's household. Now they became Keller's lifeline to the world as they spelled into her hand what was going on around her. On her eightieth birthday, Keller said she

Keller maintained her love of learning—and
helping people—to the end of her life.

would work for people with disabilities as long as she
lived, and she continued to take to the lecture platform
on occasion. She also enjoyed time with her sister in
Alabama and her brother in Texas.

In October 1961, Keller suffered the first of a
series of small strokes. For the next seven years, she
was largely confined to bed and suffered periods
of confusion.

On June 1, 1968, Keller died at her home. She
was honored in a service at the National Cathedral

in Washington, DC, where more than 1,000 people gathered to pay their respects. Afterward, her ashes were buried in the cathedral's columbarium, next to those of Sullivan and Thomson.

An Enduring Legacy

For almost her entire life, Keller had been identified by her disabilities. But she also challenged the idea of what it meant to have disabilities. By seeking an education and pursuing a career, she pushed the boundaries of what was considered an acceptable life for someone with disabilities. And she encouraged society to push those boundaries, too. "The public must learn that the blind man is neither a genius nor a freak nor an idiot. He has a mind which can be educated, a hand which can be trained, ambitions which it is right for him to strive to realize," she once said.[10]

Today, Keller's name continues to inspire. As Senator Lister Hill of Alabama said in Keller's eulogy, "She will live on. . . . Her spirit will endure as long as man can read and stories can be told of the woman who showed the world there are no boundaries to courage and faith."[11]

TIMELINE

1880
Helen Keller is born in Tuscumbia, Alabama, on June 27.

1882
In February, Keller falls ill with a severe fever that leaves her deaf and blind.

1887
Annie Sullivan arrives in Tuscumbia on March 3 to serve as Keller's teacher; on April 5, Keller learns the word *water* at the well pump and afterward begins to understand how to use language.

1888
Keller, her mother, and Sullivan make their first visit to the Perkins Institution in Boston, Massachusetts, on May 26.

1890
Keller begins oral speech lessons with Sarah Fuller of the Horace Mann School for the Deaf in the spring.

1896
Keller enters the Cambridge School for Young Ladies on October 1.

1900
Keller enters Radcliffe College in the fall.

1903
Keller's autobiography, *The Story of My Life*, is published.

1904
Keller graduates from Radcliffe College on June 28.

1905
In May, Sullivan marries John Macy, and he moves in with Keller and Sullivan in Wrentham, Massachusetts.

TIMELINE

1913
Keller and Sullivan debut on the lecture stage in Montclair, New Jersey.

1914
Polly Thomson joins Keller and Sullivan as an assistant.

1916
Keller agrees to marry Peter Fagan but is stopped by her family.

1920
Keller and Sullivan give their first vaudeville performance.

1923
Keller begins working for the American Foundation for the Blind.

1929
Midstream, a follow-up to Keller's first autobiography, is published.

1936

Sullivan dies on October 20 and Keller and Thomson soon travel to Scotland to deal with their grief.

1941

The United States enters World War II and Keller begins visiting military hospitals to talk to soldiers blinded in the war.

1946

In October, Keller and Thomson make their first trip to Europe on behalf of the American Foundation for the Overseas Blind; while abroad, they learn their house has burned down.

1960

Thomson dies on March 21.

1968

Keller dies at her home on June 1.

ESSENTIAL FACTS

Date of Birth
June 27, 1880

Place of Birth
Tuscumbia, Alabama

Date of Death
June 1, 1968

Parents
Arthur and Kate Keller

Education
Perkins Institution for the Blind
Wright-Humason School for the Deaf
Cambridge School for Young Ladies
Radcliffe College

Career Highlights
Helen Keller became the first deaf-blind person to graduate from an institution of higher learning. She achieved literary success with the publication of 13 books and hundreds of articles. She was a world-famed lecturer and performer on the vaudeville stage. Beginning in the 1920s, she worked as a fund-raiser for the American Foundation for the Blind and later traveled the world to promote the cause of the blind on behalf of the American Foundation for the Overseas Blind.

Societal Contribution

Keller worked tirelessly on behalf of the blind, raising funds and lobbying legislatures. She shared her unique perception of the world with audiences around the country through her lectures and performances. Ultimately, she changed society's perception of what it meant to have disabilities and what a person with disabilities could achieve.

Conflicts

At the age of 11, Helen faced charges of plagiarism for a story she said she had written herself. Throughout her life, critics questioned her use of words that described sights or sounds she could not possibly have experienced firsthand. She struggled to get people to listen to her views about topics other than herself and her disabilities. In 1909, Keller joined and publically promoted the Socialist Party. Many of her former supporters were appalled by her political radicalism, while others said Keller was being exploited by the socialists.

Quote

"I have the advantage of a mind trained to think, and that is the difference between myself and most people, not my blindness and their sight."—*Helen Keller*

GLOSSARY

capitalism
An economic system in which businesses are privately owned and operated for the purpose of making a profit.

columbarium
A vault with places to keep urns containing the ashes of people who have died.

industrialist
Someone who owns or manages an industry.

institutionalize
To place in a hospital or other facility for care or treatment.

lobbyist
Someone who tries to convince government officials to vote in a certain way as part of his or her job.

meningitis
An infection that causes inflammation of the membranes surrounding the brain and spinal cord and can cause fever, vomiting, headaches, and stiff neck.

pension
A regular payment made to someone, not as a wage for work.

philanthropy
The act of making charitable donations for the purpose of improving human welfare.

plagiarize

To copy and claim another person's words or ideas as your own.

rubella

A viral disease that can cause a rash, fever, and swollen lymph nodes.

scarlet fever

A bacterial disease that can cause fever, sore throat, and a red rash.

sterilize

To make physically unable to reproduce, or have children.

trachoma

A contagious eye infection that can cause blindness if not treated.

tuberculosis

An infectious disease of the lungs that can cause chest pain, fever, weight loss, and difficulty breathing.

vaudeville

A form of theatrical entertainment made up of several short, unrelated acts, such as singers, dancers, acrobats, or trained animals; popular in the United States from the 1880s to the 1920s.

ADDITIONAL RESOURCES

Selected Bibliography

Herrmann, Dorothy. *Helen Keller: A Life*. Chicago: U of Chicago P, 2007. Print.

Keller, Helen. *Midstream: My Later Life*. Garden City, NY: Doubleday, Doran, 1930. Print.

---. *The Story of My Life*. 1903. New York: Random, 2004. Print.

---. *The World I Live In*. 1908. New York: New York Review, 2003. Print.

Nielsen, Kim E. *The Radical Lives of Helen Keller*. New York: New York UP, 2004. Print.

Further Readings

Delano, Marfe Ferguson. *Helen's Eyes: A Photobiography of Annie Sullivan, Helen Keller's Teacher*. Washington, DC: National Geographic, 2008.

Garrett, Leslie. *Helen Keller*. New York: DK, 2008.

Websites

To learn more about Essential Lives, visit **booklinks.abdopublishing.com**. These links are routinely monitored and updated to provide the most current information available.

Places to Visit

Ivy Green

300 North Commons Street West

Tuscumbia, AL 35674

256-383-4006

http://www.helenkellerbirthplace.org

Ivy Green, Keller's childhood home, has been preserved and features much of the Keller family's original furniture, as well as many of Helen's personal mementos, including her braille books, braille typewriter, and souvenirs she obtained during her overseas travels. Visitors can also see the famous water pump where the world of language opened to Keller.

Perkins School for the Blind

175 North Beacon Street

Watertown, MA 02472

617-924-3434

http://www.perkins.org

Today more than 200 students are enrolled in the Perkins School for the Blind. The school is one of the few in the world that offers education geared specifically toward deaf-blind students. Tours of the campus, which features a museum dedicated to the school's history, are available to the general public.

SOURCE NOTES

Chapter 1. Mystery Revealed

1. Helen Keller. *The Story of My Life*. 1903. New York: Doubleday, 1921. *Google Book Search*, 19 Oct. 2015. 422.

2. Ibid. 23.

3. Ibid. 316.

4. Helen Keller. *The World I Live In*. 1908. New York: New York Review, 2003. Print. 72.

5. Helen Keller. *The Story of My Life*. 1903. New York: Doubleday, 1921. *Google Book Search*, 19 Oct. 2015. 316.

Chapter 2. Teacher

1. Helen Keller. "My Story." *Youth's Companion*, 4 Jan. 1894. *Disability History Museum*. Web. 19 Oct. 2015.

2. Dorothy Herrmann. *Helen Keller: A Life*. Chicago: U of Chicago P, 2007. Print. 6.

3. Helen Keller. *The Story of My Life*. 1903. New York: Doubleday, 1921. *Google Book Search*, 19 Oct. 2015. 8.

4. Joseph P. Lash. *Helen and Teacher: The Story of Helen Keller and Anne Sullivan Macy*. New York: Delacorte, 1980. Print. 44.

5. Ibid. 50.

6 Helen Keller. *The Story of My Life*. 1903. New York: Doubleday, 1921. *Google Book Search*, 19 Oct. 2015. 220.

Chapter 3. Love of Learning

1. Dorothy Herrmann. *Helen Keller: A Life*. Chicago: U of Chicago P, 2007. Print. 54.

2. Helen Keller. *The Story of My Life*. 1903. New York: Doubleday, 1921. *Google Book Search*, 19 Oct. 2015. 317.

3. Ibid. 117.

4. Joseph P. Lash. *Helen and Teacher: The Story of Helen Keller and Anne Sullivan Macy*. New York: Delacorte, 1980. Print. 77–78.

5. Helen Keller. *The Story of My Life*. 1903. New York: Doubleday, 1921. *Google Book Search*, 19 Oct. 2015. 48.

6. Dorothy Herrmann. *Helen Keller: A Life*. Chicago: U of Chicago P, 2007. Print. 63.

7. Joseph P. Lash. *Helen and Teacher: The Story of Helen Keller and Anne Sullivan Macy*. New York: Delacorte, 1980. Print. 79–80.

8. Dorothy Herrmann. *Helen Keller: A Life*. Chicago: U of Chicago P, 2007. Print. 64.

9. Helen Keller. *The Story of My Life*. 1903. New York: Doubleday, 1921. *Google Book Search*, 19 Oct. 2015. 216.

Chapter 4. The Dream of Speaking

1. *Helen Keller Souvenir No. 2 Commemorating the Harvard Final Examination for Admission to Radcliffe College, June 29–30, 1899.* Washington, DC: Volta Bureau, 1899. *Internet Archive.* Web. 19 Oct. 2015. 21.

2. "Deaf People Are Cheated by Oralism." *YouTube.* YouTube, 27 Jan. 2012. Web. 19 Oct. 2015.

3. Helen Keller. *The Story of My Life.* 1903. New York: Doubleday, 1921. *Google Book Search*, 19 Oct. 2015. 392.

4. Ibid. 414.

5. Ibid. 402.

6. Ibid. 66–67.

7. Ibid. 73.

8. Ibid. 223.

9. Dorothy Herrmann. *Helen Keller: A Life.* Chicago: U of Chicago P, 2007. Print. 90.

10. Helen Keller. *The Story of My Life.* 1903. New York: Doubleday, 1921. *Google Book Search*, 19 Oct. 2015. 201.

11. *Helen Keller Souvenir No. 2 Commemorating the Harvard Final Examination for Admission to Radcliffe College, June 29–30, 1899.* Washington, DC: Volta Bureau, 1899. *Internet Archive.* Web. 19 Oct. 2015. 23.

12. Helen Keller. *The Story of My Life.* 1903. New York: Doubleday, 1921. *Google Book Search*, 19 Oct. 2015. 226.

13. Joseph P. Lash. *Helen and Teacher: The Story of Helen Keller and Anne Sullivan Macy.* New York: Delacorte, 1980. Print. 204.

14. Dorothy Herrmann. *Helen Keller: A Life.* Chicago: U of Chicago P, 2007. Print. 95–97.

Chapter 5. Higher Education

1. Helen Keller. *Midstream: My Later Life.* Garden City, NY: Doubleday, 1930. Print. 66.

2. *Helen Keller Souvenir No. 2 Commemorating the Harvard Final Examination for Admission to Radcliffe College, June 29–30, 1899.* Washington, DC: Volta Bureau, 1899. *Internet Archive.* Web. 19 Oct. 2015. 33.

3. Joseph P. Lash. *Helen and Teacher: The Story of Helen Keller and Anne Sullivan Macy.* New York: Delacorte, 1980. Print. 221.

4. Dorothy Herrmann. *Helen Keller: A Life.* Chicago: U of Chicago P, 2007. Print. 120.

5. Ibid. 122.

6. Joseph P. Lash. *Helen and Teacher: The Story of Helen Keller and Anne Sullivan Macy.* New York: Delacorte, 1980. Print. 522.

SOURCE NOTES CONTINUED

7. Dorothy Herrmann. *Helen Keller: A Life*. Chicago: U of Chicago P, 2007. Print. 125–126.

8. Van Wyck Brooks. *Helen Keller: Sketch for a Portrait*. New York: Dutton, 1956. Print. 38.

9. Dorothy Herrmann. *Helen Keller: A Life*. Chicago: U of Chicago P, 2007. Print. 126.

10. Ibid. 131.

11. Ibid. 134–135.

12. Ibid. 126–127.

Chapter 6. Happiest Years

1. Helen Keller. *The World I Live In*. 1908. New York: New York Review, 2003. Print. 10.

2. Ibid. 177.

3. Helen Keller. *The Story of My Life*. 1903. New York: Doubleday, 1921. *Google Book Search*, 19 Oct. 2015. 21.

4. Joseph P. Lash. *Helen and Teacher: The Story of Helen Keller and Anne Sullivan Macy*. New York: Delacorte, 1980. Print. 372.

5. Ibid. 370.

6. Philip S. Foner, ed. *Helen Keller: Her Socialist Years, Writings and Speeches*. New York: International, 1967. Print. 52.

7. Joseph P. Lash. *Helen and Teacher: The Story of Helen Keller and Anne Sullivan Macy*. New York: Delacorte, 1980. Print. 458.

8. Ibid. 423.

9. Lois J. Einhorn. *Helen Keller, Public Speaker: Sightless but Seen, Deaf but Heard*. Westport, CT: Greenwood, 1998. Print. 83.

Chapter 7. Lectures and Love

1. Joseph P. Lash. *Helen and Teacher: The Story of Helen Keller and Anne Sullivan Macy*. New York: Delacorte, 1980. Print. 368.

2. Ibid. 368.

3. Dorothy Herrmann. *Helen Keller: A Life*. Chicago: U of Chicago P, 2007. Print. 147.

4. Joseph P. Lash. *Helen and Teacher: The Story of Helen Keller and Anne Sullivan Macy*. New York: Delacorte, 1980. Print. 278–279.

5. Edwin Black. *War against the Weak: Eugenics and America's Campaign to Create a Master Race*. New York: Four Walls Eight Windows, 2003. Print. 58.

6. Helen Keller. *Midstream: My Later Life*. Garden City, NY: Doubleday, 1930. Print. 182.

7. Dorothy Herrmann. *Helen Keller: A Life*. Chicago: U of Chicago P, 2007. Print. 202.

8. Ibid. 196.

9. Joseph P. Lash. *Helen and Teacher: The Story of Helen Keller and Anne Sullivan Macy*. New York: Delacorte, 1980. Print. 419.

Chapter 8. Stage and Screen

1. Dorothy Herrmann. *Helen Keller: A Life*. Chicago: U of Chicago P, 2007. Print. 223.

2. Helen Keller. *Midstream: My Later Life*. Garden City, NY: Doubleday, 1930. Print. 210.

3. Joseph P. Lash. *Helen and Teacher: The Story of Helen Keller and Anne Sullivan Macy*. New York: Delacorte, 1980. Print. 489.

4. Helen Keller. *Midstream: My Later Life*. Garden City, NY: Doubleday, 1930. Print. 224.

5. Joseph P. Lash. *Helen and Teacher: The Story of Helen Keller and Anne Sullivan Macy*. New York: Delacorte, 1980. Print. 524.

6. Ibid. 533.

7. Ibid. 530–531, 533.

8. Helen Keller. *Midstream: My Later Life*. Garden City, NY: Doubleday, 1930. Print. 68.

9. Ibid. 127.

10. Dorothy Herrmann. *Helen Keller: A Life*. Chicago: U of Chicago P, 2007. Print. 232.

Chapter 9. Later Years

1. Helen Keller. *Helen Keller's Journal: 1936–37*. Garden City, NY: Doubleday, 1938. Print. 1.

2. Joseph P. Lash. *Helen and Teacher: The Story of Helen Keller and Anne Sullivan Macy*. New York: Delacorte, 1980. Print. 537.

3. Dorothy Herrmann. *Helen Keller: A Life*. Chicago: U of Chicago P, 2007. Print. 289.

4. Ibid. 288.

5. Joseph P. Lash. *Helen and Teacher: The Story of Helen Keller and Anne Sullivan Macy*. New York: Delacorte, 1980. Print. 685.

6. Dorothy Herrmann. *Helen Keller: A Life*. Chicago: U of Chicago P, 2007. Print. 295, 290.

7. Ibid. 308.

8. Ibid. 308.

9. "Helen Keller Statue Unveiled in Capitol." *CBS News*. CBS News, 7 Oct. 2009. Web. 19 Oct. 2015.

10. Dorothy Herrmann. *Helen Keller: A Life*. Chicago: U of Chicago P, 2007. Print. 336–338.

11. "Helen Keller Biography." *American Foundation for the Blind*. American Foundation for the Blind, 2015. Web. 19 Oct. 2015.

INDEX

ABOUT THE AUTHOR

Valerie Bodden has written more than 200 nonfiction books for children. Her books have received positive reviews from *School Library Journal*, *Booklist*, *Children's Literature*, *ForeWord Magazine*, *Horn Book Guide*, *VOYA*, and *Library Media Connection*. Bodden lives in Wisconsin with her husband and four young children. Visit her online at http://www.valeriebodden.com.